JIMMY PALMIOTTI & JUSTIN

THE TATTERED MAN

written by
JUSTIN GRAY &
JIMMY PALMIOTTI

artwork by
NORBERTO FERNANDEZ

lettering & design by
BILL TORTOLINI

COVER A

ARTWORK BY:
NORBERTO FERNANDEZ

ISBN: 978-1-60706-375-9

COVER B

ARTWORK BY: **AMANDA CONNOR**
COLORS BY: **PAUL MOUNTS**

ISBN: 978-1-60706-381-0

IMAGE COMICS, INC.
Robert Kirkman - chief operating officer
Erik Larsen - chief financial officer
Todd McFarlane - president
Marc Silvestri - chief executive officer
Jim Valentino - vice-president

Eric Stephenson - publisher
Todd Martinez - sales & licensing coordinator
Sarah deLaine - pr & marketing coordinator
Branwyn Bigglestone - accounts manager
Emily Miller - administrative assistant
Jamie Parreno - marketing assistant
Kevin Yuen - digital rights coordinator
Tyler Shainline - production manager
Drew Gill - art director
Jonathan Chan - senior production artist
Monica Howard - production artist
Vincent Kukua - production artist
Jana Cook - production artist

image

UGGHHH... I'M GONNA PUKE MY GUTS OUT.

KEEP IT TOGETHER, ZEKE.

I'M SICK OKAY? SICK AS A DOG... AN IF I GET A FIX SOON... I'LL FRIGGIN' DIE!

WILL YOU SHUT UP ALREADY! WE GOTTA BE COOL HERE OR WE'LL SCREW IT ALL UP.

DING DONG

DANIKKA'S RIGHT. BE COOL. IN AND OUT AND WE'RE ON OUR WAY.

AREN'T YOU A BIT TOO OLD FOR THIS TRICK OR TREATING BUSINESS?

HEY!

GET INSIDE!

TAKE IT EASY! HE'S AN OLD MAN!

KRAK

WHAT'S THE **MEANING** OF THIS... WHAT DO YOU **WANT** FROM ME?

WHAT MAKES YOU THINK I HAVE ANYTHING OF VALUE? LOOK AROUND, I HAVE NOTHING EXPENSIVE OR **NEW**. I LIVE ON THREE HUNDRED DOLLARS A MONTH FROM SOCIAL SECURITY.

EVERYTHING. EVERYTHING YOU GOT. NOW, WHERE'S THE CASH?

HEY MAN, THIS DOESN'T **LOOK RIGHT**.

QUIET! I NEED TO **THINK.**

YOU'RE A **PENNY-PINCHING** OLD JEW.

HEY, LAY OFF THE JEW STUFF.

I **KNOW** YOU GOT SOMETHING SQUIRRELED AWAY IN HERE... MONEY, GOLD, DIAMONDS. WE WANT IT.

I DON'T HAVE MUCH... BUT WHAT I **DO** HAVE WON'T HELP YOU PEOPLE.

SHUT UP!

ZEKE, RELAX.

YOU RELAX! QUICK SCREWING AROUND OLD MAN... SHOW US WHERE THE STASH IS!

YOUR WALLET... WHERE'S YOUR WALLET?

YOU HEARD HIM!

I'VE GOT NOTHING. PLEASE...

SCREWED. WE ARE SO SCREWED.

THERE'S NO WAY WE'RE GOING TO CATCH UP WITH TYRONE IN TIME TO SCORE.

WE'VE GOT SIX HOURS BEFORE HE SAID HE WAS LEAVING! HELP ME LOOK THROUGH THIS CRAP!

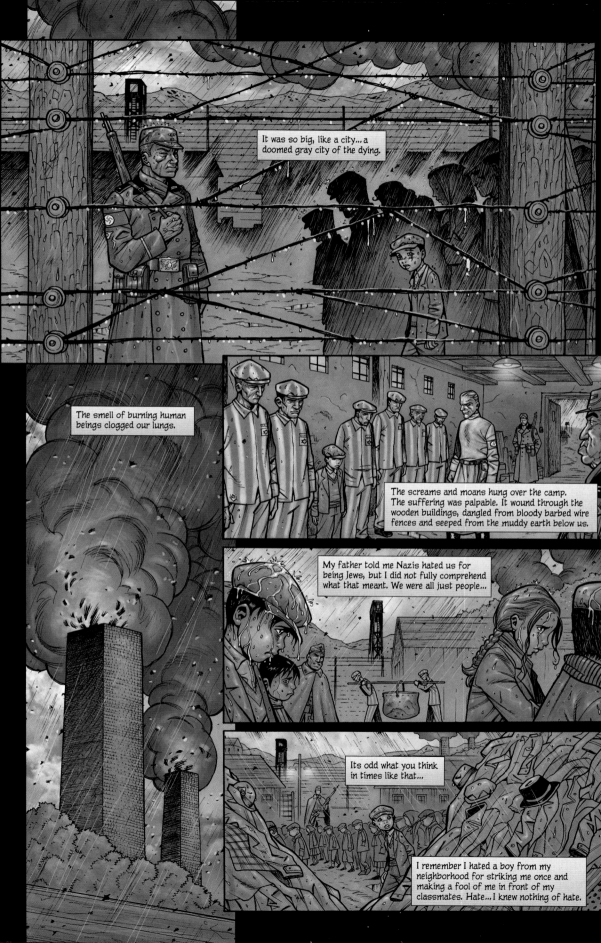

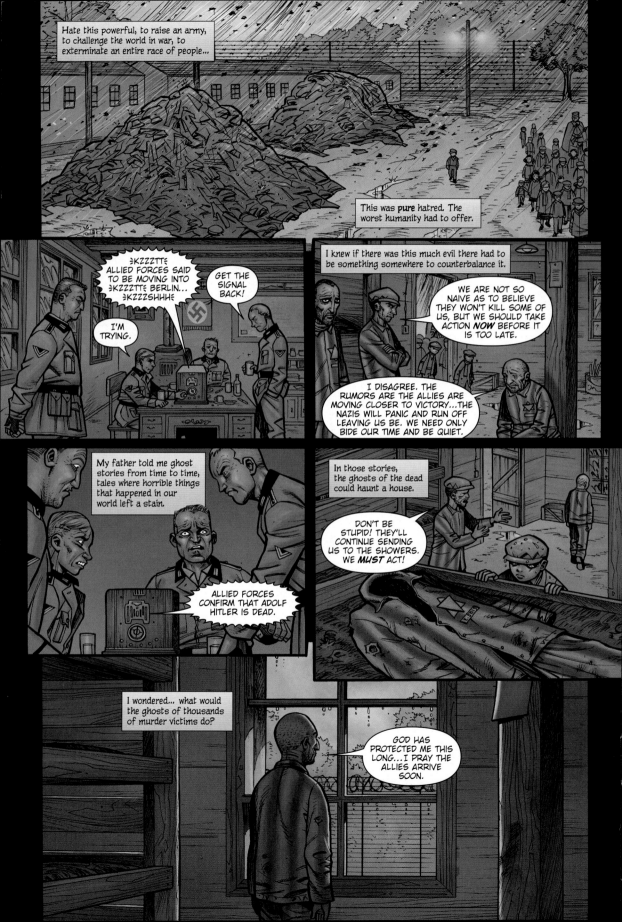

Just before dawn every man and woman in a Nazi uniform was dead.

I'll keep an eye on Danikka to make sure she's okay. Even if I can't be with her, I can still be in love with her. Monsters don't love. People do.

I never put much stock in religion. I had a Bar Mitzvah ... but when I left home I didn't honor Passover or any of the other Jewish holidays.

God never made much sense to me. I always found it difficult to believe in what I couldn't see. Now... I realize there has to be a God.

I'll continue on my path and do what must be done, but in the daylight I need my sanity.

I need the comfort and solace of something more powerful than the thing that possesses me.

Maybe I can save lives or avenge the dead, but honestly, in the end, there's only one soul I have the chance to save.

Mine...

THE END

This book exists because we had a story to tell and nowhere else to tell it.

A lot of times Justin and I get approached by all sorts of people in the entertainment business and they lean hard and heavy on us to pitch them ideas that they can develop into films or TV shows or even yet, video games. The problem we keep running into is that they really don't want anything too original. Our problem is that we don't want to do the things they suggest...and once in a while we come up with an idea that works best in the format you are now holding in your hands...a graphic novel.

The Tattered Man book is something we could continue to tell other stories of in a heartbeat. This story features all the elements of an interesting and gripping story...real emotional themes like loss, love, family, horror and above all else, vengeance. It's the story of the spirit of vengeance...how strong emotional feelings can manifest into something both magnificent and horror able at the same time. There are no good guys or bad guys here...just people making choices they have to live with and in some instances, die by. This is the kind of story I grew up reading when I was a kid...bad things happen to good people...and worse things happen to the bad. It's probably why I have such a clean cut idea what is right and wrong and why crossing both lines interests me.

When done, different people will find different characters to relate to in this story based on their own experience and that's what I love...a story where not everyones opinion will be the same. Some will love it and wish for more and some will be glad it's done and hope to never see it again and that's all o.k. In my eyes. We got to tell the story of the tattered man our way...the way we envisioned it and that's the beauty of this wonderful field we are in.

Last, I want to thank each and every one of you for giving this book a chance and believing in our work. We know there are a million other books you could be buying...but you chose ours and we want you to know how much that means to us. We put our hearts and souls in these books and hope you can see it all on display here, in the finished product.

Thanks again...and be good. The Tattered Man is watching.

Jimmy Palmiotti

I hate writing these kinds of things.

Jimmy knows that and I'm sure he finds it amusing that I'm stepping into the spotlight I so often shun.

Actually I didn't step I was gently shoved during a phone conversation when Jimmy insisted I write something for the back of The Tattered Man. Did you like it? I hope you did. I know it is a bit of a tragedy, but there's something about redemption that always strikes a chord in me. Probably because there are so few instances in life where we can truly redeem ourselves. No one is perfect and I doubt any one of you reading this could deny wanting the chance to do at least one thing over in your lives – to do it differently. I also like the idea that for some people there is no redemption regardless of what they do, but they find solace in their own actions.

The Tattered Man started as a period piece set during the second world war and evolved into a mash up of supernatural vigilantism and horror, while still trying to maintain a deep rooted hold on humanity. I don't think it is a mystery that I have an affection for the horror genre. Horror continues to thrive in the face of changing cultural tastes regardless of the generation. The reason is simple and primal - we humans are mortal and will never stop being afraid of death. On some level we're fascinated by the unanswerable question it poses. Death is an inescapable trap and the recent success of the Saw and Final Destination franchises cash in on that idea.

With the Tattered Man ,we wanted the trap to be different and the means of escape to be different as well. The horror is always on display in its truest form – what human beings are willing to do to each other. That to me is infinitely more frightening than a toothy creature reaching from the shadows. Not that I don't appreciate a good creature feature, but to be completely honest people scare me a hell of a lot more than vampires, werewolves and invisible shit on a nannycam.

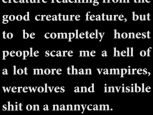

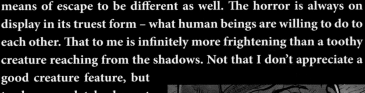

Our story's origins are in the Holocaust during Nazi Germany's campaign of terror against the Jewish people. From an existential standpoint the idea of collective suffering giving birth to something tangible isn't new. That's your basic ghost story isn't it, restless spirits tormenting the living in a quest for closure? I forget exactly what the circumstances were when I thought of it, but the idea of all those people in concentration camps being tortured and killed would make for a very big haunting. Sometimes something so horrible happens in a place that the place becomes cursed. As a period piece it would have worked, but it would have been similar to other ghost stories set in wartime. Yes, I have watched A LOT of horror movies over the last 3 decades. That gets to be tricky when you both want to create something new in that genre or enjoy it.

Taking the idea of the death trap for David in The Tattered Man being his body and soul and his only means of escape is to avenge other people's deaths and then making him homeless and living on the street during the day gave us the opportunity to develop an interesting urban legend. On behalf of the whole team that brought you this book we hope you enjoyed it and will check out some of the other indie titles we have coming up this year.

All the Best,

Justin Gray

THE TATTERED MAN
SKETCHBOOK

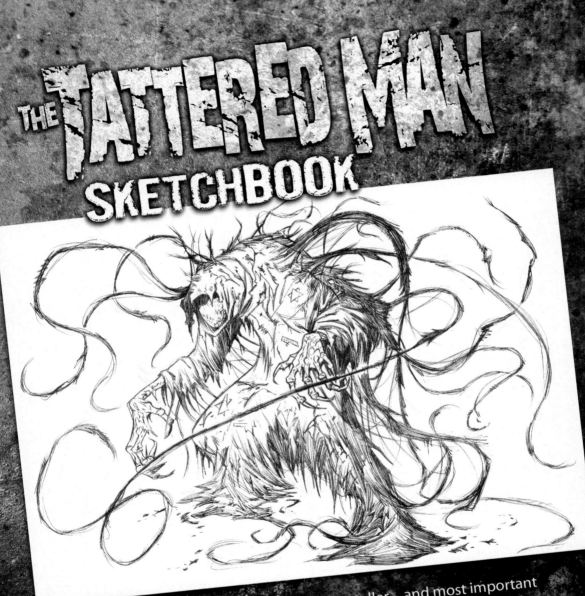

Norberto Fernandez is a brilliant artist and storyteller…and most important for us, he is a great designer. The look and feel of the main character was key in selling the concept to the reader. The Tattered Man had to be menacing and creepy at the same time, and as we described the character to Norberto…he hit us back with a few of these sketches you see here.

The first one above came back a little too "hairy" looking for us, but we loved the movement and posture…as well as the exaggerated limbs, and asked him to do a few more sketches. The next couple were spot on and are what you see featured in the story.

Honestly, at times we have to go through 15 rounds of this back and forth to get a character right, but Norberto nailed it in the second try. I told you he was brilliant.

COVERING THE COVER...

When working on the cover, we wanted something that featured all the main characters and mixed the modern story with the drab sickening past. Norberto tweaked a few different versions of this idea, including some of the characters below.

You can tell that the tattered man shape changes in some of these, as well as Norberto experimenting with a background symbol on the bottom left. In the end, we decided that the simpler open background would be best to rest the logo on.

FROM LAYOUTS TO COLOR...

The thought process of the artist is always something of interest to me. From the simple emotional elements to the final frightening finish, Norberto understood the pain and chaos that the main character was going through and presented it in quite a spectacular way.

The fifth panel is one of my favorite in the books…man, does that look like it hurts like hell. Adding just a touch of the red in the gray page gives us just the right amount of atmosphere. Wonderful.

Last, we see what an artist goes through to get to his final decisions. Imagine all the thought and choices Norberto had to go through to get to the final page. Again…a real thinking mans artist…the kind that's always a gift for us to work with.

JIMMY PALMIOTTI

Multi award-winning character creator with a wide range of experience in advertising, production, consulting, editorial, film writing, development and production, media presentation and video game development. Just a few of his clients include: Nike, Nickelodeon, Universal pictures, Disney, Warner Brothers, DreamWorks, Lion's Gate, Vidmark, Starz, Fox Atomic, Alliance films, New Line, Spike TV, MTV, 2kgames, Midway, Radical Games, Activision and THQ games.

Co-founder of such companies as Event Comics, Black Bull Media, Marvel Knights (a division of Marvel Comics), and the current Paperfilms, where he is partners with Amanda Conner and Justin Gray. Together they have created and co-created numerous universes, comics, TV series and characters including: *The New West, Monolith, 21 Down, The Resistance, The Pro, Gatecrasher, Beautiful Killer, Ash, Cloudburst, Trigger Girl 6, Thrill Seeker, Trailblazer, Ballerina, The Twilight Experiment,* and the TV series *Painkiller Jane.*

Current work includes: *Powergirl , Jonah Hex* and *Supergirl* for DC Comics, *The Last Resort* for IDW, *Back to Brooklyn* and *Random Acts of Violence* for Image Comics, and *Time Bomb* for Radical Comics.

JUSTIN GRAY

Over the last decade, Justin Gray has worked on comicbook titles that include *Power Girl, 21Down, Jonah Hex, Marvel Adventures, The Monolith* and *Daughters of the Dragon.*

He's also written for children's magazines, film, television, and video games.

Prior to his work as a professional author, Justin has been a fossil hunter, advocate for victims of crime and a microphotographer capturing rare images of of 20 million year old insects trapped in amber.

NORBERTO FERNÁNDEZ

Born in Vigo (Spain) in 1967., after some years working in a bank, Norberto made the decision to work full-time on comic books and illustration. He started working in local newspapers on strips named *Guinsy* and *Forest Hill*, written by Carlos Portela.

Later he published *Fabulas Benevolas* (at Kaleidoscope) and worked for adult magazines like Penthouse comix, Eros comix, also at *El Vibora* magazine, with the series *Broz.*

Norberto also worked on the kids magazine *Golfiño*, with the series *"El Castillo Regadera* (edited by el Patito Editorial), *Las aventuras de Xiana* and *Percy y Marionetti* (writen by David Gundin).

With Ediciones Dolmen, Norberto published the monographic called *Quatroccento*, while also working as an illustrator for books and for publicity.

Norberto has also worked at Marvel as an inker, at Zenescope doing covers.

BILL TORTOLINI

Already an accomplished Art Director and Graphic Designer, Bill began lettering comics more than a decade ago and has worked with many of comics' top creators and publishers.

Current and past projects include: *Stephen King's Talisman, Anita Blake: Vampire Hunter, Army of Darkenss, Random Acts of Violence, Cloudburst, Back to Brooklyn, The Hedge Knight, Magician: Riftwar, Battlestar Galactica, The Warriors, The Wheel of Time, The Dresden Files, Transformers, Star Trek: The Next Generation, G.I. Joe, The Last Resort,* and many others.

Bill is an avid Red Sox, Bruins and Patriots fan (and hopes Jimmy does not hold that against him). Bill lives in Billerica, Massachusetts, with his wife and three children.